Dedication

This book is dedicated to *Yeshua haMoshiach*,
Malki haShamayim -
King of the Heavens!

*Then we who are alive and remain shall be
caught up together by the Spirit to meet
Yahweh (Yeshua) in the Spirit.
And thus we shall always be with Yeshua (in eternity).*
1Thessalonians 4:17

*No one has ascended to the Heavens but He who came
down from the Heavens, that is, the Son of Man.*
John 3:13

*Yahweh Looks down from the Heavens upon the sons of men,
to see if there are any who understand,
who seek God.*
Psalm 14:2

*Do not be rash with your mouth,
and let not your heart utter anything hastily before God.
For God is in the Heavens,
and you are on Earth;
therefore let your words be few.*
Ecclesiastes 5:2

Where is Paradise?

✡ ✡ ✡

Paulette Chartrand

Razzberry Press
Arroyo Grande, CA

Where is Paradise?

Razzberry Press Edition
Perfect Bound Edition

© Abib 5996 (March-April 2015) by Paulette Chartrand

Visit our website at:
www.razzberrypress.com - A Messianic Publishing and Teaching site

Scripture verses are taken from a combination of:
The New King James Version of the Holy Bible. Copyright © 1982 by Thomas Nelson, Inc. AND The One New Man Bible, copyright © 2011 William J. Morford. Used by permission of True Potential Publishing, Inc. AND The Stone Edition of the Tanach AND My own interpretation based on the true meaning of the Hebrew words as found in the Tanach. They are copyrighted simply by being published, but Scripture is God's Word, so feel free to borrow whatever you want from the Scripture verses included in this book - they are not mine to claim.

Cover Design by Paulette Chartrand
Midnight Reflections painting by artist Anthony Casay, image courtesy of Anthony Casay Co. - website: www.casay-gallery.com

Printed in the United States of America 2015

ISBN-10: 0 - 9824591 - 6 - 5
ISBN-13: 978 - 0 - 9824591 - 6 - 4

Where is Paradise?

✡ ✡ ✡

Paulette Chartrand

Table of Contents

Glossary of Hebrew Words

Glossary of Hebrew Words

The Names of the first five Books of the Bible

English	Hebrew	Pronunciation	Actual Translation
Genesis	Bereshit	Bear-a-sheet	In the beginning
Exodus	Shemot	Shem-mote	Names
Leviticus	Vayikra	Vy-eek-ra	And God called
Numbers	Bemidbar	B'-mid-bar	In the wilderness
Deuteronomy	Devarim	Dev-var-eem	Words

Some of God's Names

English	Hebrew	Pronunciation
Light of the World	Or goyim	Or go-yeem
God the Redeemer	Elohim ha goel	El-o-heem ha go-el
God of our Salvation	El Yeshu-atenu	El Yesh-oo-ah-tay-noo
God our Deliverer	El Yeshuati	El Yesh-oo-ah-tee
God the Faithful	El hanne eman	El hahn-nay ay-mon
God our Father	Elohim Avinu	El-o-heem Ah-vee-noo
God of my Strength	El Sali	El Sah-lee
All Sufficient God	El Shaddai	El Sha-dye
Holy One of Israel	Kedosh Yisrael	Khay-doesh Yees-ra-el
Presence of God	Paniym Elohim	Pah-neem El-o-heem
Lord	Adonai	Ah-doe-niy
Our Creator	Yahweh	Yah-hweh
Lord of hosts	Yahweh tsevaot	Yah-hweh tsay-va-ote
Our holy God	El Kadosh	El Kah-doesh
Salvation	Yeshua	Yesh-shu-ah

Introduction

Introduction

Revelation

Like most believers, I had always believed that people go to Heaven when they die. And I *knew* that it was just a *temporary holding place* until the Earth was restored, where we would live out eternity with Yeshua. But I had never studied the Scriptures concerning this so-called *fact*. Then recently one morning, I woke up with the words in my heart, *"You don't go to Heaven when you die."*

Of course my mind responded, "We don't? Then where do we go?" Then, I asked Yeshua to show me this *new revelation*, and thus began my search into the Scriptures to find the truth about *Heaven*. Because He led me to discover where *Paradise* really is, I had to put the book I was working on aside in order to verify that I had been hearing correctly from God by searching His Word. This wasn't anything I had ever really thought about or studied before.

I began to dig deep into the Hebrew words of *Paradise*, *Heaven* and many others, and soon realized I had to find the **proof** in the Scriptures of where *Paradise* really is - and share it with you.

Popular Teachings

Contrary to popular teachings and beliefs, Paradise is **_not_** Heaven. It is an age-old *dream* of the devil to ascend to the *Heavens*, **where God lives**. Isaiah 14 and Ezekiel 28 tell us the devil's desire. He is the one who has told us we too can go to the *Heavens* - God's home. This is also a Greek concept, and has crept into both the Jewish and Christian concepts of the afterlife. So we must search the Scriptures to find what it actually states.

Rabbinic Talmudic study delves too much into Greek mystic ideals, and these are lain over the Scriptures causing the result to be so far off what God had in mind, one cannot see the real truth.

Christians rely too much on Greek interpretations of the Scriptures, which is completely contrary to the Hebrew Mind Who wrote, and *is* the *Word of God*. These interpretations are Greek beliefs that are exactly like the lies of the desires of the devil - they desire to go to Heaven to be like God. And we have been convinced we can go live in God's home, too - **without any Scripture to back it up**.

The Rabbis and the Christians rely completely on philosophies and teachings filled with error that have been passed down for two thousand years or more, *rather than relying on what the Word of God actually states*. Philosophy is nothing but a bunch of theories of one or more particular philosophers, concerning the study of a theoretical basis of a particular branch of knowledge or experience. That theory then creates an attitude held by a person or organization that acts as a guiding principle for beliefs and behavior. This is not truth, it is conjecture.

Instead of conjecture or popular teachings, I chose to search through the Scriptures to find the truth about *Paradise*. I think many of you will be surprised because you have been taught that Heaven and Paradise are one and the same place. But there is nothing in Scripture to back up this claim. My searching uncovered some amazing facts and truths unknown to most.

What this book will do is lay out the facts as shown in the Scriptures. Each chapter will show facts concerning the title of the chapter. All chapters will lead up to the truth, which will be revealed in the next to the last chapter, called *So Where in the Universe is Paradise?* This *final* chapter will use those facts to show us where Paradise really is.

You *could* sneak a peek at this *last* chapter first, but it is the chapters leading up to it that will reveal the truth in the Scriptures. Not only do I use the Hebrew words, but also Scripture itself, to prove that we do **not** go to Heaven when we die. But do not lose heart, because we *do* go somewhere very special to God.

The Heavens is God's Home

Chapter One

The Heavens is God's Home

According to Scripture, God is the only One Who lives in the Heavens (but we also know that the angels can go there too). **There is nothing in Scripture stating Heaven is where the *righteous dead* go.** The Heavens is God's home, not ours, nor is it our *goal* or *reward*.

In Luke 16:26 Abraham is speaking to the rich man who is asking to come where Lazarus is, and says, "*And besides all this, between us and you there is a great gulf fixed, so that those who want to pass from here to you cannot, nor can those from there pass to us.*"

The *gulf* speaks of the *abyss*, as in the pit of hell (or lake of fire). *Abraham's bosom* is not in the Heavens. The Heavens is not that close to hell. This *gulf* seems to be between the pit of hell and wherever *Abraham's bosom* is, and we know that hell is here on Earth - or rather, under the Earth (Bemidbar 16:30-33 & Psalm 55:15).

"*But if Yahweh creates a new thing and the earth opens its mouth and swallows them up with all that belongs to them, and they go down alive into the pit, then you will understand that these men have rejected Yahweh.*

Then it came to pass, as he finished speaking all these words that the ground split apart under them, and the earth opened its mouth and swallowed them up, with their households and all the men with Korah, and all their goods.

*So they and all those with them went down alive into the **pit**, the earth closed over them, and they perished from among the congregation.*" Bemidbar 16:30-33

The Hebrew word for **pit** here is **sheol** which means **hades** or **the world of the dead.** So this is definitely speaking of what we call in English, **hell.** So yes, hell is under the earth. These men were rebellious men and God knew their hearts would not change.

Going Up or God Coming Down?

Never once in Scripture has God requested us to come up to Him to **His home** in the Heavens; neither did He promise us a life in the Heavens with Him. What He says is that we will be with Him **in eternity** (Romans 6:23) - which is somewhere on this Earth, and it will be forever.

The Earth was made for us, and it is where we will always live (Psalm 115:16), so why would God then bring us up to His home where we won't be able to live?

Yeshua's shedding His blood for us does not work for us in the Heavens. He offered His blood on the altar in the Heavens, but that is because He lives there and that is where the true altar is.

Earth is mankind's home, and the Heavens is God's home. **Yeshua atoned for our sin here on Earth**, not so we can go to the Heavens, but because then it would be possible for us to live eternally with Him here on **Earth**.

God comes *down* to us in several instances. He does not want us in the Heavens, nor can He have us there because our sinful nature will not allow us to live in the Heavens, God's home. Because He is holy, God could not be near His Temple on Earth when there was sin present (Ezekiel 8:6), therefore it is the same today.

Note: A very interesting fact is that Yeshua provided a way for Himself to *tolerate sin* here on the Earth - He had to do that so that His Spirit could live inside a human being. However, we are still unable to be with Him in the Heavens - He must preserve His own home from sinful mankind because He is holy.

The Heavens & the Earth

Psalm 115:16 states that the Heavens belong to God, but the earth was given to mankind.

Psalm 138:8 and Amos 9:2 are not speaking of actually going to the Heavens - they are metaphors within the context of speaking of how big God is.

Proverbs 30:4 speaks of God being the only One Who can ascend or descend to and from the Heavens.

Ecclesiastes 5:2 states that God is in the Heavens and mankind is on Earth.

The devil has continually caused mankind to think he can ascend to the Heavens, as we see in Isaiah 14:13 and Ezekiel 28:2. The devil is the one who desires to be like God, and it is he who causes us to believe that we can go to God's home in the Heavens.

Isaiah 14:12 is speaking of the devil himself as he fell from the Heavens (but the chapter is about the king of Babylon). In Ezekiel 28 God is speaking to the king of Tyre. These verses are speaking of mankind as the devil influences them.

Ponder this: Since only God lives on the Heavens and Elijah was taken up in God's chariot, then if Elijah was actually taken *up* in God's Chariot, then it is highly likely that Elijah is Yeshua (2Kings 2:1).

Rewards & Treasures

Matthew 5:12 states that our *reward* is in the Heavens, and we have always assumed that means we will collect it when we get there. But what this really means is that our *reward* will **come from** the *Heavens* when it is time to receive it. We will not go to collect it, it will come to us here on Earth.

Everything in the Hebrew Scriptures that *comes from* the Heavens, states that it *comes from the Heavens* or *that it is in the Heavens* - never in Scripture does it say one goes to the Heavens to retrieve it.

Matthew 6:19-21 is not speaking of earthly material things, it is speaking of the *things of God*. Remember, the word *Heaven* (as in *Kingdom of Heaven*) is synonymous with *God*. So if our hearts and focus are on Yeshua, then we will receive Godly wisdom and guidance - not *treasures* as in real Earthly treasures. We have taken our English words too literally when God was speaking of *spiritual* things.

The Greek word for *treasure* is *thesauros*, and mistakenly shows in the Strong's as *a deposit* or *wealth*. But when you look up the root word, which is *theo*, you find a completely different meaning. It means *to prostrate oneself*. So **our treasure is God**, and when our focus is on God, which will in turn bring our hearts to God, then all we will want to do is worship Him. *We will come before Him on bended knee to prostrate ourselves before Him - our Treasure.*

But lets take a look at the *Hebrew* word for *treasure* also, which is *otsar*. It actually means *storehouse*, as in *God's storehouse*. It is from the root word *atsar* which means *to store up*. But we have a very wrong concept of what God's storehouse is or has in it. **His storehouse is full of *the things of God***, and we need only ask Him for knowledge of Himself and He will show us whatever we ask of Him. **Our treasure is God.**

> **Note:** We must remember that Yahweh, in the flesh of Yeshua, *brought the Kingdom of the Heavens to the Earth*, and that is what the verses in Matthew are speaking of. The *Kingdom of the Heavens* is synonymous with *God*, or *Kingdom of God*. It speaks of God.

The Greek word for *reward* is *misthos* and means *payment for service*. The Hebrew word for *reward* is *shalam* and is the root for *shalom*. It means *to complete* or *restore*, or *deliver* or *finish*.

So our *reward laid up for us on the Heavens* is for us *when the Earth is restored*. *Our <u>reward</u> is the <u>deliverance</u> we received by faith when we accepted Yeshua as our Savior and Messiah*.

Deliverance is *our payment for the service of worshiping Yeshua*. It is our gift from God. The meaning of *reward laid up for us on the Heavens* is that it is coming *from* God - because <u>*the Heavens is God*</u>. **Our reward is God**.

If you have received the information in *this book*, and also the information in the *I AM the Way* book, and of course the *Hebrew Scriptures*, then you have received your *reward* and your *treasure*.

You have been given *treasure* beyond what you could imagine because you have been given God's *gift of deliverance* - something none of us deserve. And your *reward* is *being blessed with this knowledge* - knowledge only a few will have at the end of the ages.

Where Do Angels Live?

Chapter Two

Where Do Angels Live?

This chapter is to clear up some misconceptions about angels based on false teachings about them - both from pulpits in churches, and those heathens who claim to have knowledge about angels. Any teaching that cannot be found within the Hebrew words of Scripture is false.

The Hebrew language is where we find the Truth in Scripture, and we should not trust only in our English words. On the surface, our English words may not show certain information, but the Hebrew words will in fact reveal things that are clearly there right before our eyes. This chapter will also show where angels actually *reside*.

False Teachings About Angels

In my research for information on angels, besides what is in the Scriptures, I ran across a website that stated that it is not mentioned in the Bible that angels have wings. This same person also stated that angels are merely people, and do not actually live in the Heavens. There was much more information that is completely inaccurate, but the statement about ***wings*** alone shows just how ignorant some people can be - but claim to be experts on a subject.

Just on the first subject about angels not having wings, two or three verses come to mind just off the top of my head, that prove this statement to be false: Isaiah 6:2 and Ezekiel 1:11 and Revelation 4:8 where the **Seraphim** are being described (the Hebrew word *seraph* means *a flame or fire* and is referring to *flaming angels*) - just one kind of angel that is in fact mentioned in Scripture as having wings. As you can see, this description about this one type of angel can be found in both the Hebrew Scriptures and the New Testament.

1Kings 6:24, 1Kings 8:6 and 2Chronicles 3:13 are a few more verses that clearly state that angels, in this case the Cherubim, have wings. Although it is speaking of the Cherubs that were carved in wood in the Temple, clearly God had to have shown Moshe what a Cherub looks like in order for him to be able to carve and/or make these living creatures. And Revelation 9:9 speaks of the *sound* of the wings of the angels.

I believe 1Corinthians 15:42-44 is where some (false) teachers of the Word have gotten the idea that people become angels when they die. Somehow these false teachers have gotten the idea that a *spiritual body* is the same as an angel. But this *spiritual body* that Shaul is speaking of is what we are when our spirits come back to life (when we accept Yeshua into our lives). It has nothing to do with *becoming* angels (something else mentioned on that site mentioned above).

An angel is a spirit being, but just as there are different types of angels, there are also different types of spirit beings. Angels are only one type of spirit beings, and they are very different than humans. Angels do not have a mortal human body - although they apparently can appear as people to us. Humans are spirits, but human spirits have flesh and blood bodies. Angels do not have flesh and blood bodies, and we know this by the Hebrew word used for angels, which is *malak*. *Malak* is a *messenger* (angel) of God - the ancient meaning of the letters *mem-lamed-alef-chet*, being *mighty controller of the Leader's fence of protection* (the angels do God's work of protection).

For a human spirit (with a flesh and blood body), the Hebrew word *nefesh* is used, the ancient meaning of the letters *nun-fey-shin*, being the *destroyer begins life* (of a human spirit) - the Destroyer being God.

People do NOT become angels when they die, and the Bible does in fact mention that angels *do* have wings. So clearly, the person who wrote the information on that website mentioned above, and those who teach false things about angels, never actually check to see if their facts are true. They never read or consult the Bible or they did not research it enough to find the true meaning behind certain words.

Much of the information on the internet is not true and we must be discerning when reading anything on the web. You must look up those things mentioned on websites, and I even expect you to look up the verses I mention in this book so you will know for sure if the information presented here is true.

So Where *Do* the Angels Live?

So, now lets look to see what *is* in the Bible about angels. Where do they live? We need to take a look at certain facts to discover this. Bereshit 28:12 speaks of the angels ascending and descending a ladder in Jacob's dream. The ladder reached to the Heavens, so obviously the angels are allowed to *go* to the Heavens, and Earth.

In Bereshit 32:1 and Matthew 22:30 we can see that these beings are called **angels of God**. These are God's creatures, and we've already established that it is God Who lives in the Heavens. So do the angels live there with Him?

In Matthew 24:36 these creatures are called **angels of the Heavens**. Mark 12:25 calls them **angels in the Heavens**. The Bible does speak of the evil angels (angels who have sinned) *leaving their proper domain* (Jude 6), and 2Peter 2:4 speaks of the evil angels who have been in chains in Tartarus (deepest abyss of hell or hades; or to be incarcerated in eternal torment). But these evil angels no longer live in the Heavens (Revelation 12:9).

Now that we know where the evil angels no longer live, how about those two thirds of the angels who still have access to the Heavens? Take a look at Luke 2:13 where it speaks of the *heavenly host*. This *Heavenly Host* are an army of angels.

Tsevaot is the Hebrew word translated as *hosts*. This word has a modern ending, so what we find in the Strong's Concordance is *tsabaah* or *tsavaah*. It can mean simply an *army* in some verses, but wherever it reads as *Yahweh of hosts* (*Lord of hosts* in our Bibles) it is actually speaking of an *army* of *angels* (*tsavaah* is a singular word, whereas *tsevaot* is a plural word). It is this **heavenly host** who will return with Yeshua - not believers who were never in the Heavens.

In 2Kings 21:3 we are told that Manasseh rebuilt the *high places* (place for heathen worship of idols). He worshipped the *host of the heavens* - as in the **angel armies of the Heavens**. It was a common heathen practice to worship the stars, the angels or anything of creation - rather than the Creator.

So I think we have established where the angels come from, and therefore they reside there, too - **in the Heavens with God**. The Heavens is God's home, and it is where the angels minister to Him. Although they do come to Earth and minster to us humans on Earth as well, they do not reside on Earth.

Translation Error

In Psalm 8:5, Hebrews 2:7 & 9, both the Hebrew and the Greek word that is translated as *angels* has been translated incorrectly. The word is *Elohim*, which means *God*. It has never meant *angels* and never will. ***Yeshua was made a little lower than <u>God</u>*** (not the angels), so He could die for mankind.

Because of this mistranslation, many have a misguided idea of the difference between angels and people. And it also gives us a misguided idea of Yeshua being a completely different being than God.

This mistranslation was actually done by the Hebrew Sages because they couldn't comprehend Someone (Yeshua) being in the same category as God (not knowing He is God). So they deliberately put Him in the same category as angels instead - and the 15th century translators copied this.

Garden of Eden

Chapter Three
Garden of Eden

Many believe the Garden was destroyed by the Flood. But in truth, it's actual location on the globe can never be established on this corrupt Earth, so it is a waste of time to try and find it. **Scripture clearly states that God hid Eden** (Bereshit 3:24), therefore it is still in the same geographical location where the Bible states it is. The Flood did not wipe Eden off the map - nor was it moved.

The rivers mentioned in several places in Bereshit, as well as in Daniel when he speaks of the river Heddekel while in captivity in Babylonia, has caused many to believe Eden was originally in Iraq. But there has never been any proof that the rivers mentioned in Bereshit are actually the rivers we think they are today.

The Hebrew Word, Eden

Let's take a look at the ancient meaning of the Hebrew letters that form the Hebrew word *Eden*: **ayin-dalet-nun**. *Ayin* means *to see, to experience* or *understand*. *Dalet* means *Way* or *Door*. *Nun* means *Life* or *action*. So the ancient meaning is: *to see the Way of Life*. In other words, one *experiences* or *sees God's Way of Life* when they are in the place we call *Eden*. These letters can also mean *eternal Life*.

We find the deeper meaning of *Eden* when we look at its root words, of which there are two: *Eden* is from the root words *ed*, which means a "*set period of time*" or "*temporary*," and from *ood* (ayin-yod-dalet), which means *to be duplicated*, as in *to be restored*. This is quite a unique meaning. **Eden** has been set for *a specific period of time to be restored* - with the Earth.

But then we must also look at **qedem** or **qedmah**, the Hebrew words used for **East**, as in **East** *of Eden* or **East** *in Eden*. This is another word that cannot quite be translated into English and do it justice as far as God's meaning goes. But the closest I can come is that it also has an **eternal** quality, making **East** and **Eden eternal**. This word for **East** also means **before**, as in **Eden** was **before** - or even **before time**. The **entrance** to the Tabernacle and Temple faced **East**.

We are told in the Scriptures that God planted a **Garden** in Eden, and the Hebrew word **gan** (*garden*) means *a park, field* or *forest*. Some even believe its meaning is closer to an **enclosure**. But according to the ancient meaning of its letters, this **Garden** will be **restored to its original state and location (East)**, when the **Earth** is **restored to** *its* **original state**.

The Hebrew Word Paradise

The Greek word for **Paradise** is **paradeisos**, and means *a par*k or *forest*. It means the same as the Hebrew **pardes** (originally a Persian word): *a park, orchard* or *forest*.

The **Heavens** has **never** been referred to in Scripture as *a park, field, orchard* or *forest*. This is the description of **gan Eden** (garden of Eden). So when Yeshua told one of the thieves that he *would be with Him in Paradise*, Yeshua was not speaking of the **Heavens** - He was speaking of **Eden**.

Ezekiel's Eden

Many people believe the *Eden* mentioned in Ezekiel is not the same *Eden* as in Bereshit. But Ezekiel is speaking of the same *Eden* that we read about in Bereshit; and he is also speaking of a *future Eden* - that which will be restored (and revealed) at the end of the ages - and is one and the same as the Eden in Bereshit.

Several of the prophets, if not all, prophesied in many different *times*: **past, present and future all at the same time** within their prophecies. That is why we cannot tell in the English of which *time* they are speaking. We must look up the Hebrew words to find those *secrets*.

The Proximity of Eden and Hell

Luke 16 speaks of *a great gulf* between *Abraham's bosom* and hell. *Abraham's bosom* is not the **Heavens**, but judging by the description here, it is on Earth - because we know that hell is on Earth (under the Earth, as mentioned in a previous chapter).

Even the Talmud speaks of Eden and Hell being pretty close to each other (see chapter Four). If this gulf is between the pit of hell and Abraham's Bosom and Abraham's Bosom is Eden, then Eden is here on Earth, and so is the lake of fire (hell).

The Jewish View of Afterlife

Chapter Four
The Jewish View of Afterlife

Jewish Thought on the Afterlife

Although the Rabbis teach that there isn't much on the afterlife in Scripture, we know that Abraham believed in the resurrection of the dead, because his faith in Isaac being raised from the dead depended on this belief. So in the other chapters we take a look at the whole Torah, even *before* Abraham's time to find information on what God actually says about His people living with Him in eternity.

For the most part, it is the Rabbis eyes that have been veiled to the Truth within the Scriptures, which causes them in turn to debate and create false teachings based on philosophies, and ultimately pass them on to other Jews. So what you are about to read in *this* chapter is based on Greek philosophy, confused debating and unfortunately, pure fabrication based on Scripture verses that have nothing to do with the afterlife.

The Rabbis claim that the Torah is quite vague about life after death. And most of their beliefs are based on Greek ideas, from about 300BC and later.

According to the Talmud, there are a nether Gehinnom and an upper one, over against the nether and the upper Gan Eden. Curiously enough, in this *theory* hell and paradise adjoin each other. One Rabbi claims that a partition of only a hand-breadth, or four inches wide, separates them. The Rabbis say the width is but two fingers according to the Talmud. In the Talmud Rabbi Akiba said: "Every man born has two places reserved for him: one in paradise, and one in Gehinnom. If he be righteous he gets his own place and that of his wicked neighbor in paradise; if he be wicked he gets his own place and that of his righteous neighbor in Gehinnom."

The question "Who may be a candidate for either Gehinnom or paradise?" is solved by the *majority rule*. If the majority of the acts of the individual are praiseworthy, he enters paradise; if wicked, he goes to Gehinnom; and if they are equal, God mercifully removes one wicked act and places it in the scale of good deeds. The Talmud deduces the immortality of the *soul* from the Scripture verses Ecclesiastes 12:7, Isaiah 57:2 and I Samuel 25:29.

The Rabbis are almost unanimous in maintaining that there is a terrestrial, as well as a celestial Gan Eden. The Garden of Eden in Genesis is supposedly a model in miniature of the higher Gan Eden called *Paradise*.

Paradise is occasionally referred to as *Olam ha-Ba*, which the Rabbis say means *the world to come* (but the word *olam* means *eternity* or *forever*). Generally the term *Olam ha-ba* is used for the post-millennial time, after the Messianic and resurrection periods. Sometimes the terms *Gan Eden* and *Olam ha-Ba* are interchanged.

In the Talmud, *Gan Eden* is recognized by Naḥmanides as *Olam ha-Neshamot (the world of the souls)*, which the departed souls of the righteous enter immediately after death.

In the Middle Ages, however, most of the people and many rabbis failed to grasp this Jewish *spiritual* meaning of *paradise*, and accepted all haggadic references in a literal sense. Maimonides was probably the first *authority* to strike a blow at this *literalness*, by asserting in unmistakable terms the fallacy of such a belief. "To believe so," he says, "is to be a schoolboy who expects nuts and sweetmeats as compensation for his studies. Celestial pleasures can be neither measured nor comprehended by a mortal being, any more than the blind can distinguish colors or the deaf appreciate music."

Maimonides maintains that the Gan Eden is terrestrial, and will be discovered at the millennium (Maimonides, Commentary on Sanhedrin 10). This view evoked considerable opposition from the contemporary French rabbis; but the Spanish rabbis, especially Naḥmanides, defended Maimonides except that of his theory of punishment after death.

Gan Eden at the End of Days

Bereshit 13:10: *"And Lot lifted his eyes and saw all the plain of Jordan, that it was well watered everywhere (before Yahweh destroyed Sodom and Gomorrah) like the garden of Yahweh, like the land of Egypt as you go toward Zoar."*

Joel 2:3: *"...The land is like the Garden of Eden before them, and behind them a desolate wilderness."*

Isaiah 51:3: *"He will make her wilderness like Eden and her desert like the garden of Yahweh."*

Many times throughout Scripture, a land, usually Israel, is compared to Eden. In Isaiah we see that Israel will become like Eden, not only in the near future several times, but also at the end of the ages.

The Vagueness of the Rabbis

The ancient rabbis often talked about Gan Eden as a place where righteous people go after they die. However, it is unclear whether they believed that souls would journey to Gan Eden directly after death, or whether they went there at some point in the future, or even whether it was the resurrected dead who would inhabit Gan Eden at the end of time.

One example of this vagueness can be seen in Exodus Rabbah 15:7 (Talmud reference), which states: "In the Messianic Age, God will establish peace for the *nations* and they will sit at ease and eat in Gan Eden."

While it may be apparent that the rabbis are discussing Gan Eden at the end of days, this quote does not reference the dead in any way. Therefore we can only use our best judgment in determining whether the *nations* they talk about are righteous souls, living people or the resurrected dead. One author believes that in this excerpt the rabbis are referring to a *paradise* that will be inhabited by the righteous resurrected. His basis for this interpretation is the strength of the rabbinic belief in resurrection when Olam Ha Ba arrives. Of course, this interpretation applies to Olam Ha Ba in the Messianic Age, not Olam Ha Ba as in the afterlife.

Gan Eden as an Afterlife Realm

Other rabbinic texts discuss Gan Eden as a place where souls go immediately after a person dies. Barakhot 28b in the Talmud relates the story of Rabbi Yohanan ben Zakkai on his deathbed. Just before he passes away ben Zakkai wonders whether he will enter Gan Eden or Gehenna, saying "There are two roads before me, one leading to Gan

Eden and the other to Gehenna, and I do not know by which I shall be taken." Here you can see that ben Zakkai is talking about both Gan Eden and Gehenna as afterlife realms and that he believes he will immediately enter one of them when he dies.

Gan Eden is often linked to Gehenna, which was thought of as a place of punishment for unrighteous souls. One Jewish teaching says, "Why has God created Gan Eden and Gehenna? That one might deliver from the other" (Pesikta de-Rav Kahana 30, 19b). The rabbis believed that those who studied Torah and led a righteous life would go to Gan Eden after they died. Those who neglected the Torah and led unrighteous lives would go to Gehenna, though usually only long enough for their souls to be cleansed before moving on to Gan Eden.

> **Note:** The rabbis' idea of *studying Torah*, was actually studying the Talmud - the supposed *hedge* around the Torah.

Gan Eden as an Earthly Garden

Talmudic teachings about Gan Eden as an earthly paradise are based upon Genesis 2:10-14 which describes the garden as if it were a known location:

*"A river watering the garden flowed from Eden; from there it was separated into four headwaters. The name of the first is the **Pishon**; it winds through the entire land of Havilah, where there is gold. (The gold of that land is good; aromatic resin and onyx are also there.) The name of the second river is the **Gihon**; it winds through the entire land of Cush. The name of the third river is the **Hiddekel**; it runs along the east side of Ashur. And the fourth river is the **Perat**."*

Notice how this passage names the rivers and even comments upon the quality of gold mined in that area. Based upon references like this the rabbis sometimes talked about Gan Eden in Earthly terms, debating whether it was in Israel, Arabia or Africa (Erubin 19a), because of where it is mentioned the rivers *run*. They likewise discussed whether Gan Eden existed prior to Creation or whether it was created on the third day of Creation.

Much later Jewish mystical texts describe Gan Eden in physical detail, detailing "gates of ruby, by which stand sixty myriads of ministering angels" and even describing the process by which a righteous person is greeted when they arrive at Gan Eden. The Tree of Life stands in the center with its branches covering the entire garden and it contains "five hundred thousand varieties of fruit all differing in appearance and taste" (Yalkut Shimoni, Bereshit 20).

In another teaching the students and rabbis would follow the pattern of PARDES (Jewish interpretation), because they believed that *such study would lead them to paradise which they interpreted as the Garden of Eden*. The sages believed that when Adam and Eve were cast out of the Garden of Eden that God put an angel armed with a *flaming sword* at the gate to prevent anyone from entering (Bereshit 3:23-24).

In Dresh (a part of PARDES) it is learned that the ancient Hebrew expression, *flaming sword*, really means *to create an illusion* (*flaming* is the Hebrew word *lahat*, meaning *to blaze* but also with the idea of *enwrapping something covertly in enchantment*; and *sword* is *chereb* which means *to cause desolation by a sharp instrument*, as in causing Eden to become *a place of desolation* - deserted of people). God created an illusion that the Garden of Eden no longer existed. Yet, if given insight into the supernatural world one will be able to see the Garden of Eden and actually enter it. It is felt that this is where Enoch went as *he walked with Yahweh and was no more* (Bereshit 5:24).

The Garden of Eden is often referred to as *Abraham's Bosom*, a place where the souls of the righteous go until the Messiah comes to redeem them. According to the Talmud, only the truly righteous may enter *Pardes*, or the Garden of Eden - *Abraham's Bosom*.

The Afterlife in Scripture

Although the Rabbis claim that the Bible is vague on the afterlife, there are several places that give us hints that Scripture does indeed speak of it.

In Daniel 12:13 the angel is telling Daniel that *he will arise to his inheritance at the end of days*.

In Job 42:10 it states that Yahweh restored Job's losses and gave him twice as much as he had before. Yet in verse 42:13 it states that Job had seven sons and three daughters when Yahweh restored his losses. This is the same number of children Job had at the beginning. The only way Job could be given *twice as much* as he had before is that these other children that had died *would arise at the end of days*.

Isaiah 42:9 hints at an afterlife in saying that the *old things have passed*, and that *new things will spring forth*. We know this because Isaiah is a prophet who often spoke in the past, present and future all at the same time.

In Psalm 23:7 this famous Psalm ends with *"and I will dwell in the house of Yahweh forever."*

Psalm 139:23-24 David is telling Yahweh to test him, and asking Yahweh to *"lead me in Your Way forever."*

Proverbs 10:25 tells us that the *"righteous have an eternal foundation."*

Eternity & Eternal Life

Chapter Five
Eternity & Eternal Life

Many people believe the Hebrew Scriptures do not tell us much about eternity or eternal life, but as mentioned in the previous chapter, there are many places in Scripture that speak of this very thing. The New Testament speaks of it so often because the authors are only quoting from the Hebrew Scriptures. So if they are quoting from what they learned in the Torah, then yes, the Torah does indeed speak of eternal life.

There are several places where God makes *eternal promises* to His people in the Hebrew Scriptures. To name a few, Bereshit 9:16 and Psalm 105:10 where the *eternal Covenant* God made between Himself and His people is mentioned. Bereshit 17:8 and 48:4 where the *eternal possession* of the land of Israel is mentioned. Shemot 40:15 where the *eternal priesthood* is mentioned. Vayikra 16:34 speaks of an *eternal statute*. In Isaiah 56:5 God's everlasting Name is spoken of. Isaiah 45:17 tells us that there is *eternal salvation*. And in Habakkuk 3:6 *God's Way* is *eternal*.

An *eternal covenant*, *eternal possession*, *eternal priesthood*, an *eternal statute* and *eternal salvation,* and of course *God's Way* all imply that there will be *eternal life* for God's people - you can't have these *eternal* things without God's people. *God's Way* is *eternal* because it was designed specifically for life for His people. And this *eternal life* will be spent on the *Restored Earth*.

Eternal Life

Throughout the four gospels, Yeshua continually reminded us that if we believe in Him, we will not see death - *eternal death* (John 5:24 & 29). We are spirits with flesh and blood bodies, and as believers in Yeshua we are to believe in *eternity*. We are to live our lives expecting to live eternally with Yeshua, because we are *eternal spirits*. But do we really believe *eternal life* is real?

Some consider death to be the lack of eternity, but *eternal life* implies that there is something that lies beyond death. Our spirits are eternal wherever we end up - we will either spend eternity with Yeshua, or we will spend it in a place our English translates as *hell* - a place of eternal torment. 2Corinthians tells us that our spirits are indeed eternal, and those things which we can see will eventually disappear, but *those things that are eternal will materialize at the end of the age when the Earth is restored*.

"*We do not despair on account of this, yet if indeed our outer man is corrupted, then **the one within us (spirit) is being renewed day by day**. Truly our affliction for the moment is insignificant beyond measure and proportion into eternal fullness, a **weight of glory eternally working out in us**, we do not notice what we are seeing, but the things we do not see. For the things we see are temporary, but **the things we do not see are eternal**.*" (2Corinthians 4:16-18 ONMB)

Words of Eternity

Taking a look at what Scripture says about *eternity* we find many different words in English. The main Hebrew word for *eternity* in the

Bible is *olam,* and is usually translated as *everlasting*, *perpetual* or *forever*. *Olam* can also mean *universe*, because the universe is eternal - without end. Some even call it *world without end*.

A couple of other interesting words (both mean the same thing), that we have already discussed in a previous chapter, is *qedem* or *qedmah* and both are usually translated as **East**, but it implies that *East* means *eternal*, as in *East of Eden has no end*.

But lets take a closer look at these Hebrew words. There is *olam* which can mean *concealing, eternal, always, continuance, without end, perpetual, everlasting* and *evermore*.

As just mentioned above, *qedem* or *qedmah* mean *Eastward* or *East, but imply an eternal element,* such as *before time,* or *everlasting*.

And then we have *evermore* which is the word *netsach*, and means *a goal, continually,* or *perpetual.* Other places in the Scriptures we can find these words are 2Samuel 22:51, 1Chronicles 17:14 and in Psalms 37:27, 106:31 and 133:3.

Eternity as a Place

In Isaiah 57:15 it is implied that *eternity may be the place where God dwells*, rather than a particular *place in time*. The Hebrew word used is *shekem*, which is generally translated as *a habitation*, but can also mean *to continue* - or *a habitation which continues without end*.

In most Bible translations, it states *"For thus says the High and Lofty One, Who **inhabits** eternity, whose name is Holy...,"* but in the Tanach it states, *"For thus said the exalted and uplifted One, Who abides forever and Whose Name is holy..."*

Two completely different statements, but the Hebrew words can mean either statement. The word used in this verse for *eternity* or *forever* is *ad*, which also means *continuity*, *perpetual*, *forever* or *eternity*. The Tanach is the only Bible that states otherwise. As you can see, *it is highly possible that <u>eternity</u> is indeed where God dwells*.

The Restored Earth

Isaiah 65:17, Revelation 21:1 and 21:5 all speak of the *Restored Earth*. Our Bibles show *new* Earth, but the Hebrew word that is generally translated as *new* is *chadashah*, and the Greek word is *kainos*. Although our Bibles use the word *new* as a translation for both of these words, both of these words actually mean *<u>to restore</u>*, with the Hebrew word being a little more descriptive: *to restore to a previous condition*.

And so the Earth will be *restored* to what is once was - just as perfect as Eden once was (Isaiah 51:3) - and will be again. The Earth will no longer be corrupt and sin will be gone, and Eden will no longer be hidden. The Earth will be eternal, as will all believers. And we will live with Yeshua *eternally* on the Earth.

Everlasting and *forever*...believe in *eternal life* for it is very true!

Jewish vs Greek Heavens

Chapter Six

Hebrew vs Greek Heavens

Hebrew vs Greek

There are two major types of cultures and thought, both past and present. There is the **East**, which is Hebrew, such as all Middle Eastern nations. The other is **West** which is Greek, such as what you find in Europe and America. Both of these cultures view their surroundings, lives and purposes in ways that would seem foreign to the other.

Ancient Greek thought views the world through the mind, or *abstract thought*. A Greek mind views man as constantly changing and evolving, and therefore God must be changing with him. *Ancient Greek thought* is how most of mankind thinks and acts today. Our view of the Heavens today is very Greek, so we must rethink the facts about the Heavens - and of course, search and check the Scriptures.

Ancient Hebrew thought viewed the world through the senses, which is known as *concrete thought* - the expression of concepts and ideas in ways that can be seen, touched, smelled, tasted or heard. In other words, all five senses were used when speaking, hearing, writing or reading the Hebrew language. The Hebrew idea of the Heavens was originally the knowledge that God and His angels are the only ones who live in the Heavens. But since the Greek invasion, the Hebrew idea of the Heavens has changed considerably (see Chapter Four).

Greek Spirituality

The spiritual world around us is most definitely *otherworldy*, but we actually live in the very Earthly world that exists inside this *otherworldly bubble*. This Earthly world on which we live is that which God created. So, although we are spiritual beings, because we also have a flesh and blood body, *being spiritual* **is actually lived out on this Earth**.

But Greek thinking would have us strive to be in that otherworldly world, or rather Heaven. The Greek word *proskairos* is usually translated as *temporary* or *temporal*. This very Greek term can only be found in one place in our Bibles (2Corinthians 4:18). *Temporary* and *temporal* are related to time, as in *a short time* - **but this verse is speaking of our _short lifespan_ on this earth.** In Greek thinking it is the Earth as our home that is considered *temporary*.

The verse where this word ***proskairos*** can be found has been twisted to reflect the Greek ideal of our lives here on Earth. It tells us that our lives on this Earth are temporary because we are going to Heaven. This Greek teaching tells us we are not *citizens* of Earth, but of Heaven - so our true home is Heaven.

But in reality 2Corinthians 4:18 is **_not_** speaking of Earth being our temporary home. Earth is our permanent home, **it is the <u>bodies</u> we live in that are <u>temporary</u>**. God made the Earth, and this is where He wants to dwell with us. Earth is our permanent home - we live on Earth and will eventually live on the Restored Earth.

God never expected us to come up to Him, nor does He want us to. **He actually came down to the Earth** to live among us: first with Adam and Chavah, then in the Tabernacle, in the Temple, as Yeshua and then He provided a way for His Spirit to dwell inside each one of us - _on the Earth_. **He wants to dwell with us here on Earth.**

When the end of this age comes, we will still be living on this Earth God gave us - it will be restored to its incorruptible condition, much like Eden originally was (Ezekiel 36:37). The Earth is our home and it is where God wants to live with us.

As mentioned earlier, to continually try to reach an (impossible) plane of _otherworldliness_ is very Greek, and actually contrary to our very Hebrew God. The Greeks continually tried to attain a place outside of this world because to them an _otherworldly feeling_ made them _feel_ more superior and spiritual. They were always trying to reach out to where the gods lived - they thought to live in the world of the gods would please the gods. They were always trying to please gods who really couldn't care less about their lives on this earth - because, of course, they weren't real. Because of continually trying to reach Heaven, the Greeks thought very little of life here on Earth. To continually desire to leave this life on Earth, which is a gift from God, is not only a Greek idea, it is contrary to the Torah of God and the mind of God. AND it is the goal of the enemy, who will use anything and everything to cause one to rebel against God.

Rewards & Inheritance

The New Testament tells us that our **rewards** and our **inheritance** are in the Heavens, but it never states that we must go there to retrieve it. It simply means that our rewards and inheritance are coming **from** the Heavens. It is the teachings of our churches that has caused us to believe these **rewards** and **inheritance** are things we will obtain when we *get to Heaven.* This teaching is not in Scripture, nor in the New Testament.

Our very Hebrew God created this Earth, and gave it to us. He created us *from* this earth, and so He expects us to live in it, work in it and use it to create Godly things, and to take care of it.

Life is not about reaching for the stars or an otherworldly existence, it is about thoroughly enjoying the creation God gave us for our home. To use it as He intended it to be used. God gave us this *Way of Life* (Torah) because we live on earth, not in the Heavens. Earth is our home, and God's *Way of Life* was specifically designed for life on Earth - the corrupt Earth.

Earth is not a temporary home, as we have been taught. We must train ourselves to change our Greek ideas about the Heavens. We are to use the earth, and its resources. We are to tap into the Spirit Who lives inside us, not so we can leave our bodies, but so we can be guided to live full lives on this very Earth. The Earth will be restored to what it once was as we read that the garden in Eden was in Bereshit, so we will still be living on this Earth even into eternity.

Souls of Mankind

Chapter Seven

Souls of Mankind

The Hebrew word **nefesh** is generally translated as *soul* (or life), but it actually means **a spirit with a flesh and blood body**. So in reality, a *soul* is not really a *soul*. The *soul* is a Greek abstract concept.

So what does it mean to be a *spirit with a flesh and blood body*? Where do these **spirits with flesh and blood bodies** go when they die? Where will they live in eternity? We can know the answers to all of these questions if we tap into the Living Spirit that lives inside us - Yeshua.

Our *spirits with a flesh and blood body* are walking around with Yeshua's Spirit living inside them. We are to emulate God's Spirit, and this in turn transforms our own spirits, giving us the Hebrew mind of Messiah.

Instead of believing what we are told by well-meaning teachers, Yeshua wants to show us Himself what is in His Scriptures concerning this subject. He speaks to our *souls* (the **hearts** of our spirits with a flesh and blood body), and in turn our hearts speak to our own minds.

We tend to forget that Yeshua actually lives inside us, so we think all our thoughts are our own thoughts. But if you have been studying God's Word, celebrating His Feasts, and His Sabbaths (on Saturday), then you are being transformed daily. And most likely your thoughts are not your own thoughts - they are the thoughts of Yeshua. So yes, you are definitely hearing God even when you don't realize it!

The Mind of Messiah

Those thoughts that are Yeshua's thoughts are from a very Hebrew mind. To have *the mind of Messiah* (1Corinthians 2:16), or *let this mind be in you* (Philippians 2:5) actually means something quite different than what we have been taught. The Greek words for mind are *phroneo* or *nous*, both more accurately translated as *a thought process* - which should be defined as a *Hebrew thought process*.

In the Hebrew Scriptures the word *mind* does not exist because it is an abstract word, and abstract words have no place in Hebrew thought or Scripture. There are three main Hebrew words used in Scripture that are generally translated as the English word *mind*: *lev* (heart), *ruach* (spirit) and *nefesh* (life or soul). Based on these words, it is the *Spirit of Messiah*, or the *Heart of Messiah* or even the *Life or Soul of Messiah* that we are to possess or imitate on this very Earthly world. This paints a completely different picture than the Greek picture. **This is a very Hebrew picture, and it is *God's Heart, Soul* and *Spirit* that we have within us while we are alive.**

The Earthly World

The Earthly world is that which we can see, hear, touch, taste and smell - those things we experience with our five senses. It is through these five senses that we witness God in our world, and we commune with Him too. Earth is the world God has created for all the *spirits of mankind* to live in. Our very Hebrew God created this Earth and gave it to us.

This Earthly world is what the New Testament derogatorily calls *natural*, but this is where we live - on the Earth that God created and gave us. According to Scripture, it is where God intended all spirits of mankind to live, eternally.

The Word of God continually tells us to trust in the Word, and in what God tells us will keep us in good health, in safety and in a warm home. The Bible is actually something that God gave us in the Earthly world, and it is filled with His Godly wisdom. Yeshua actually gave us an ***instruction book*** on how to live on this corrupt Earth, because Earth is our home.

God says to not worry about what we will need in this Earthly world - ***He will take care of all our needs***. He will work for us in a very *super-Earthly* way - if we will let Him. All Yeshua ever wanted was for us to worship Him and trust Him to take care of us - on Earth.

The Spiritual World We Live In

God is the Spirit of all spirits. These other *spirits* live in the spiritual realm that surrounds the Earth. We too are spirits (*with flesh and blood bodies*) surrounded by that same spiritual realm. Although we cannot see into the spiritual realm, we are definitely sharing our *space* with spiritual beings who live in the realm that surrounds our Earthly world - spirits of Light *and* of darkness.

Believers are spirits with Light - the Light of God, Who is Yeshua living inside them so that they radiate His Light. And His Light leads us to more light, and so on. Angels also have the Light of God.

The *souls* of mankind must be in constant communion with the Father (Yeshua) to be prepared at all times: keep God's Commandments, and read and study His Torah continually.

What Yeshua wants to ultimately do for us, is to give us His full Power on this Earth. On the Earthly world in the first century, there were no restrictions on the believers - they were so tuned into the Spirit of God within them, that they literally walked like Yeshua did on the Earth. But that changed with the venture into error at the end of the first century: false doctrines and false teachings. God is now in the process of correcting all these errors, but because believers are not *in sync* with God yet (still very much in error), we still have restrictions.

God made the Earth for mankind to live on, to take care of, and for Him to come and live with us. Earth was made for the ***souls of mankind***, and the Heavens were made for Yeshua.

The Heavens

Chapter Eight
The Heavens

Heavens is always plural in Hebrew, which some have taken to mean that there are different *levels* of Heaven. Based on Talmudic teachings, there are *seven levels of Heaven*, and apparently Christian writers borrowed this (false) teaching, even to the extent of adding 2Corinthians 12:2 in the fourth century. This chapter is sufficient without this verse, and makes a lot more sense without it too. We've already established that *Paradise is not the Heavens*, so while *this man was caught up in the Spirit to see Paradise* (2Corintians 12:3-4), he was not caught up into the *Heavens*, especially not a *third Heaven* that does not exist.

In one of my Bibles there is an appendix in the back about the *seven levels of Heaven* which are based on *seven words* that refer to God's dwelling place, or the Heavens. **In reality, there are about fourteen different words used in Hebrew to describe the Heavens, and not one verse where these words are found refers to being a *level* of the *Heavens* in Scripture.**

While some of these words describe a certain type of element in the sky, or parts of the Heavens, they are not *levels*. Several of them describe the same parts of the Heavens, so it most definitely causes doubt about the so-called *levels*. We must remember that God is a plural God, therefore His home is plural also - and He is synonymous with the Heavens. They are Echad (One) because God is Echad (One).

All in all, these words do in fact describe God's habitation, which is the **Heavens**. I have often thought that Heaven was a sphere, like the Earth, because that is what Enoch1 states; and I had the Greek idea that we humans would go to live on this *sphere* called Heaven.

But God is so big, and the universe is only a part of Who He is - God is Spirit, so He dwells anywhere and everywhere all at once. Yeshua is His human form, and it is this form that we often think of when we think of where He lives. But God can be everywhere and anywhere all at the same time, so when He is home in the Heavens, God is not in human form. But **His human form can also manifest here on Earth, even *while* He is at home in the Heavens**.

We humans tend to think of things only in our own understanding. God's habitation is the universe and beyond, and even eternity. Some believe God's *glory* is where He dwells (kabod, hadar, hode, tifarah), but His **glory** is ***Who He is***: *majesty*, *beauty* and *honor*, to name a few of His attributes - and the definition of these Hebrew words that mean **glory**.

We really cannot comprehend all Who God is, where He dwells and who we are *in Him*. But to narrow these thoughts down to God's home, we're going to take a look at each of the fourteen words in Hebrew to give us a better understanding of God's home, *the Heavens*.

Doq - Isaiah 40:22

*"It is He Who sits above the circle of the earth, and its inhabitants are like grasshoppers, Who stretches out the Heavens like a **curtain**, and spreads them out like a tent to dwell in."*

Doq is considered to be the *entire universe*, and goes beyond what we can see with telescopes. This is the word that is translated as *curtain*, but is more accurately translated as *crumbling powder, or fine dust or vapor - with an appearance as a thin cloth*.

The ancient meaning of the Hebrew letters in *doq* (dalet-kuf) is *what follows the Door (or Way)*. It is almost as if the fine dust or vapor is *what follows in the wake of the Way* as He goes by, and we know that we have just seen God when we look into the Heavens.

Raqiya - Genesis 1:17

*"And God set them in the **firmament** of the Heavens to give light upon the Earth."*

Raqiya could be a reference to the stars, sun, moon and planets. The *outer space* is where the various heavenly bodies move in their prescribed orbits, maintaining relationships in constellations, solar systems and galaxies. *Raqiya* is from the root word *raqa* which means *to expand by hammering*; to *overlay* or *make broad*, *to spread* or *stretch*.

According to some, *Raqiya* is the part of the Heavens that we call the *expanse*, or visible *arch of the sky* - that which can be seen with the naked eye. *Raqiya* is the word that is usually translated as *firmament*.

The ancient meaning of the Hebrew letters in *Raqiya* (resh-kuf-yod-ayin) is *what follows the Highest Hand of Knowledge*. Again, we have a sort of *trail* that follows God when we *see* Him in the Heavens.

Shachaq - Psalm 78:23, 24

*"Yet He had commanded the **clouds** above, and opened the doors of the Heavens, had rained down manna on them to eat, and given them of the grain of the Heavens."*

This is where the Rabbis believe the millstones are located that grind manna (grain from the Heavens) to be rained down for God's people. *Shechakim* (plural of *shachaq*) is said to be the *atmosphere*.

Shachaq is usually translated as *skies* or *clouds*. This word actually means a *a powder as in a small heavenly dust or vapor* - such as accumulating into *clouds*. It is from the root word of the same name, which means *reduced to minute particles or fragments*.

Shachaq is the *clouds*. But *Raqia* means pretty much the same thing, so we must take this into consideration when we hear explanations that cannot be found in Scripture.

The ancient meaning of the Hebrew letters in *shachaq* (shin-chet-kuf) is *what follows the consumed (or destroyed) separation*. In other words, the dust or vapor is separated but God gathers it all together to form the clouds in His Heavens.

Zebul - Isaiah 63:15

*"Look down from the Heavens and behold from the **habitation** of Your holiness and of Your glory!..."*

Zebul is translated as *habitation*. We know that *Zebul* is a *dwelling place* for God's glory, because Isaiah is speaking of God looking down from *the Heavens*, from His *habitation*.

The ancient meaning of the Hebrew letters in *zebul* (zayin-bet-lamed) is ***the house of the sword that pierces***. This means when we allow God to pierce our hearts in order to mold us into His willing vessels, He does it from ***His Habitation***, the Heavens. But He is also living within us, so it also comes from within ***His other Habitation***, us.

Maon - Psalm 26:8

*"Yahweh, I have loved the **habitation** of Your house, and the place where Your glory dwells."*

Maon is describing God's tabernacle or temple here on Earth in this verse, but Devarim 26:15 tells us that this word *maon* speaks of God's *holy habitation* in the Heavens.

*"Look down from your **holy habitation**, from the Heavens, and bless Your people Israel and the land which You have given us, just as You swore to our fathers, 'a land flowing with milk and honey.'"*

So we know that the Earthly Tabernacle and Temple were not only copies of God's Home in the Heavens, they are connected too.

The ancient meaning of the Hebrew letters for *Maon* (mem-ayin-vav-nun) is ***blood (water) of knowledge is joined to life***. Blood is Covenant, the water of knowledge is Torah and Life is Yeshua. The Heavens are tied to Yeshua and all that He is - and they are His home.

Otsar - Devarim 28:12

*"Yahweh will open to you His **storehouses**, the Heavens, to give the rain to your land in its season, and to bless all the work of your hand..."*

As mentioned in Chapter One, the Hebrew word for **treasure** is *otsar*. It means **storehouse**, as in **God's storehouse**. This word is translated as both **storehouse** and **treasure**, but the English meanings of these words is completely different than what the Author intended.

Otsar is from the root word **atsar** which means **to store up**. Our concept of what God's storehouse is or has in it is nothing like reality - **His storehouse is full of _the things of God_**, and we need only ask Him and He will show us whatever we ask of Him. Our *treasure* or *storehouse* is God because **God, treasure, storehouse** and the **Heavens** are all interchangeable.

Otsar is supposedly the location of the storehouses of snow, rain, hail, whirlwinds, storms. Job 38:22 uses this word *otsar* in a manner where we can see that God refers to the **_treasure_ _of snow_** and the **_treasure_ _of hail_** - those things that come from His Heavens. And so it is highly possible this is a part of the Heavens where these **treasures of snow and hail** do come from.

The ancient meaning of the Hebrew letters of *otsar* (alef-vav-tsade-resh) is **joined to the strong inescapable Man.** Our treasure is God, therefore even the snow and the hail of the Heavens is joined to Him.

Anan - Isaiah 19:1

*"Behold, Yahweh rides on a swift **cloud**, and will come into Egypt; the idols of Egypt will shake at His presence, and the heart of Egypt will melt in its midst."*

Here **anan** is translated as **cloud**. It is said that here in **anan** is where righteousness, judgement and charity, the storehouses of life, of peace and blessing, the spirits of the righteous, and Yahweh will hereafter revive the dead to live with Him here. And supposedly the angels live here too.

BUT, this is all Jewish conjecture, and we have already established that the righteous dead do not go to the Heavens, where God dwells.

Isaiah 18:4 tells us that this **cloud** is a part of God's habitation, *"For so the Lord said unto me, I will take my rest, and I will consider in my **dwelling place** like a clear heat upon herbs, and like a cloud of dew in the heat of harvest."* There is also another aspect we must consider about **anan** - it is a **thunder cloud** or **nimbus cloud**.

The ancient meaning of the Hebrew letters of **anan** (ayin-nun-nun) is **see the life of action**, as this thunder cloud is very active and seems to have a life of its own. But of course we know that the clouds, even the **thunder clouds** are God's **habitation**.

Navah - Exodus 15:13

*"You in Your mercy have led forth the people whom You have redeemed, You have guided them in Your strength to Your **holy habitation**."*

This verse is in the midst of the Song of Moses, right after the Egyptians were swallowed up by the Reed Sea. So God was not living in the Tabernacle yet. I believe this word **navah** is speaking of *eternity*, which in other places it is hinted that *eternity* is God's **holy habitation**.

Navah is *a home* or *residence*, and most times is translated as **habitation**. It implies **rest** and **beauty, to celebrate with praises** and *a pleasant place*. *Eden* is often translated as *a pleasant place*.

The ancient meaning of the Hebrew letters of *navah* (nun-vav-hey) is *what comes from the action of the nail* - in other words, our rest in Yeshua is because He allowed Himself to be nailed to the cross. His rest is our rest. It can also mean our own *death* in Messiah.

Yashab - Psalm 110:1

"Yahweh said to my Lord, 'Inhabit My Right Hand till I make Your enemies Your footstool.'"

Yashab is translated as *to abide*, *to dwell*, *habitation* or *to inhabit*. We also find this word translated into the Greek word *hemai* in Hebrews 1:13. Although this word also means *to dwell* or *to inhabit*, the English translation used *sit down*, because of the confusion over Who Yeshua really is, and over what *sit down* in this case really means. *To set and position Yourself to inhabit* is a more accurate translation of the Hebrew word *yashab*. Hebrews 1:13 is a quote from the above Psalm.

The ancient meaning of the letters of *yashab* (yod-shin-bet) is the *Hand of the consumed house*. God's *Hand* consumes His home making it His habitation - *to inhabit it* is *to consume it*. And *IT* is *His Right Hand* - the *Right Hand of Power*, where He dwells.

Chaziyz - Zechariah 10:1

"Ask rain of Yahweh in the time of the latter rain, so Yahweh will make flashes of lightning and give them showers of rain, grass in the field for everyone." (ONMB)

Chaziyz is translated as **glare** or **a flash of lightning**, **a bright cloud** or **lightning**. I'd say this is obviously a part of the **Heavens** where lightning comes from, and we know that lightning is God's presence, or how He is manifested here on Earth when He comes down from the **Heavens** (Exodus 20:18).

The ancient meaning of the letters of *chaziyz* (chet-zayin-yod-zayin) is **to separate and pierce with the hand weapon (sword)**. This *latter rain* is Yeshua - i.e. Salvation. Salvation causes a believer to be separate and then Yeshua pierces our hearts and uses His Sword (the Word) to create willing vessels for Himself. This **lighting** is the Word and it comes from the Heavens.

Shamayim - 2Chronicles 6:39

*"Then hear from the **Heavens**, Your dwelling place, their prayer and their supplications and maintain their cause, and forgive Your people who have sinned against You."*

Shamayim is from the root word **shameh**, which means **lofty**, the **sky** as in **aloft**, or the **visible arch in which the clouds move**. But it is also where the **higher celestial bodies revolve**. **Shamayim** is the most often used word in Hebrew to refer to the **Heavens**.

The ancient meaning of the letters in **Shamayim** (shin-mem-yod-mem) means **to consume the waters** (**mayim** means **waters**). In other words, **God is all consuming of the waters of the Heavens** - He is everywhere all at once. His habitation is **haShamayim** (the Heavens). **Shamayim** can also mean **to destroy the waters**, as in separating the waters of the Heavens from the waters of the Earth.

Ariyf - Isaiah 5:30

"*And in that day they shall roar against them like the roaring of the sea: and if one look unto the land, behold darkness and sorrow, and the light is darkened in the* **heavens** *thereof.*" KJV

Ariyf is from the root word *araf*, meaning *to droop* or *drip*. It is referring to the sky as *it droops at the horizon of the Heavens*. This is a lowering and increasingly dark sky that is ready to *drop* its weight of water.

The ancient meaning of the letters in *ariyf* (ayin-resh-yod-fey) is *see the work of the Voice of the Highest*. When we look up at this darkening sky, *we see God at work* - it rains because enough water vapor has gone up from the oceans to gather in the Heavens to form rain clouds. While we take everything that happens on this Earth for granted, God, His Heavens and His creation never stop working.

Arabah - Psalm 68:4

"*Sing unto God, sing praises to his name: extol him that rideth upon the* **heavens** *by his name Yah, and rejoice before him.*" KJV

Arabah is from the root word *arab*, which means the *dusky evening sky with a sense of sterility*. As in the *sterile valley of the Jordan* - the *sterile desert* or *wilderness*. It refers to the *Heavens as they darken*. Most translations use the English word *clouds*, but the King James Version actually has the closest true translation which is the *Heavens*.

The ancient meaning of the Hebrew letters in *arabah* (ayin-resh-bet-hey) is *what comes from seeing the House (Temple) Man*. This *sterile sky in the Heavens* can be compared to our very *sterile* God, Yeshua, Who is *uncontaminated, pure* and *unblemished - sterile*.

Maiyn - Devarim 26:15

*"Look down from Your holy **habitation** from the **Heavens**, and bless Your people Israel and the land which You have given us, just as You swore to our fathers, 'a land flowing with milk and honey.'"*

Maiyn is similar in meaning to *maon*, and thus is translated as *habitation* here (the same verse was used for *maon*). Even though the Strong's concordance states this *habitation* is God's Tabernacle or Temple, we can see clearly in this verse that it is speaking of the *Heavens*. On the other hand, *God's Tabernacle or Temple are One with the Heavens*, thus they are tied to the Heavens.

The ancient meaning of the Hebrew letters of *maiyn* (mem-ayin-yod-nun) is a little different than *maon*, and is the *blood (water) of knowledge is the action of the Hand*. Again, *the Heavens and God are synonymous*, so what we see the *Heavens doing* is *God doing*. The Heavens are God's habitation because *He is the Heavens*. As mentioned before, *Yeshua's Blood* is Covenant, *water of knowledge* is Torah and Life, and they are all Yeshua. The *Heavens* are tied to Yeshua and all that He is.

Keep in mind that most of the *assumptions* of the *seven levels of Heaven* are from Rabbinic origins. The Rabbis have conjured up many false things about God - those things that came as a result of the very confusing debates within Rabbinic Judaism. We must look to the Scriptures for the Truth - not the Talmud (Rabbinic teachings).

Several of the above words do not actually speak of God's *habitation*, but they do speak of the different parts of the *Heavens* - and the *Heavens are God's home*.

Totality of it All

These words not only describe the different parts of the Heavens, they are also different descriptions of all that is the Heavens - and the totality of it all is God's Home.

So Where in the Universe

is Paradise?

Chapter Nine

So Where in the Universe is Paradise?

The Flood in Noach's time changed the surface of the Earth dramatically, so much so that the *Four Rivers* spoken of in Bereshit may not be in the same places, nor actually flow from the same places. It is highly possible that these four rivers originally flowed from Israel.

On the other hand, Eden is still in the same place, but hidden. Many are constantly trying to locate Eden from the descriptions in Bereshit, but we simply will not be able to find it this way, nor any way. God has hidden the **Garden** until the *End of the Ages*.

The word **Paradise** is derived from a Persian word and came to be in existence some time shortly after the Babylonian exile. With the Persians now in rule over the Israelites, and false teachings running rampant even after they were allowed to return to Jerusalem, the Israelites adopted many Persian things.

They not only picked up on calling God the *King of Heaven*, they also began to refer to the place where the righteous dead go as *Paradise*, the Persian word being *Pardes*, which eventually became a modern Hebrew word, and ultimately our English word *Paradise*.

Later, after the Greek invasion of Israel, the ancient Hebrews soon adopted many of the Greek ideas of gods and Heaven. The ancient Greeks believed that people's souls go to Heaven when they die, and therefore so did the Hebrews. This was carried over into the manmade religions of Judaism and Christianity (please see *I AM the Way, The*

Essentials of God's Way: The Last Move of God for the explanation of this statement).

Our belief system is based on Greek ideas, but everything in the Scriptures is purely Hebrew. Given this information you have read so far, where in the world (literally) is Paradise?

Paradise has long been thought to be one and the same as Heaven, but as I will show you in this chapter, and as you have seen in the previous chapters, it is **not** the *Heavens* this Paradise speaks of.

It's All Greek to Me

The Greek word for **heavenly**, **epouranios**, is a very misunderstood word. In each case the word **heavenly** is used, it is not speaking of actually being in the Heavens, as most have misunderstood its meaning to be. It simply means something akin *to bringing the Heavenly down to the earth*, as **being in the same time and space as the Heavens - but on Earth**. But it is not speaking of *being in* or *going to*, the Heavens.

Epouranios uses the prefix **epi**, which very interestingly, means **to be in the same time and space**, as in **superimposition**. In other words, this prefix gives the word **ouranos** (usually translated as *heaven*) a completely different meaning than simply, **ouranos** (*belonging to* or *coming from the sky*, but implicates **eternity** rather than the *Heavens*).

But what about 1Thessalonians 4:17?

*"Then we who are alive and remain shall be **caught up** together with them in the **clouds** to **meet** Yahweh (Yeshua) in the **air...**"*

<u>The literal translated Greek, word for word:</u>

*"Then we the living who remain together with them shall be **caught away** in the **air meeting** Yahweh (Yeshua) in the **air** ..."*

We cannot take this literally by the English words. We must look up the Greek words, and then find the equivalent Hebrew words. The key words in this verse are: **air** and **caught away** and **meet** (the word **clouds** is not even in this sentence).

Greek for *air* is *aer* and means *to blow* or *breathe* (has absolutely nothing to do with clouds or air). It was translated from the Hebrew *ruach* which means *wind, to breathe, to blow* - or <u>*spirit*</u>.

Greek for **caught up** is *harpazo* (a derivative of *haircomai*) which means **to seize** or **take by force**. *Haircomai* means *to take for oneself* or *to prefer*. Harpazo is from **airo** = *to lift* or *to raise*; *to remove* or <u>*expiate sin*</u>, and is comparable to the Hebrew words *nerd* or *nerah*, which mean *aromatic*, and is from the root word *ner*, meaning a *lamp* or *light*.

Greek for *meet* is *apantao* or *apantesis*, which usually means *an encounter*. But it is from *apo*, which has numerous meanings, but it has been discovered that in most cases it means *by* or *because of*.

<u>And so the actual translation of 1Thessalonians 4:17 is:</u>

*"Those who have had **sin removed** by Yeshua, will be **taken for Himself** by **His Spirit, because of** His Spirit dwelling (encountering our spirits) inside us."* (This *taking* will appear much like the smoke going up from the lamp of God, and will be a *sweet aroma* to Yeshua.)

To be taken *by God's Spirit* is very real - it is *not* something like a dream or vision. It really happens. Anytime someone in the Bible mentions being *taken in the Spirit* they are speaking of something that literally happened to them. We somehow think this means in our minds, but *in the Spirit* is a **physical** thing that happens.

This is what will happen to those who are ready for Him, when Yeshua returns to *take* us. We will **not** meet Him in the air or in the clouds. We will be *taken to Eden* (which is on Earth) by God's Spirit - He will not be taking us to the Heavens. The *Heavens* is God's home, not ours.

And what about 2Corinthians 12:2 & 4:

*"I know a man in Messiah who fourteen years ago (whether in the body I do not know. or whether out of the body I do not know, God knows) such a one was caught up to the **third heaven**. And I know....how he was **caught up** into Paradise and heard inexpressible words, which it is not lawful for a man to utter."*

The literal translated Greek, word for word:
*"I know a man in Messiah years ago fourteen, (whether in the body I know not, or out of the body I know not, God knows) **caught away** such a one to **third heaven**. And I know.....that he was **caught away** to Paradise, and heard unutterable sayings, which it is not permitted for man to speak."*

Caught up or *away* is the same word as used in the above example, *harpazo* - it means *to take by force for Himself*, and this *taking* is *as the smoke of the lamp of God going up,* making *a sweet aroma to Him*.

Third heaven is ***tritos ouranos***. As mentioned earlier, the word ***ouranos*** is usually translated as ***heaven***, but the implication is closer to ***eternity***. As pointed out in a previous chapter, this ***third heaven*** cannot be backed up in the Hebrew Scriptures. It does not exist. I believe the "*third heaven*" line was added in the fourth century, as well as the part in parenthesis, because there is no such thing as "*out of the body*." So this verse should have read:

"*I know a man in Messiah years ago fourteen, that he was caught away to Paradise and heard unutterable sayings, which it is not permitted for man to speak.*"

The Rivers

"*A river watering the garden flowed from Eden; from there it was separated into four headwaters. The name of the first is the **Pishon**; it winds through the entire land of Havilah, where there is gold. (The gold of that land is good; aromatic resin and onyx are also there.) The name of the second river is the **Gihon**; it winds through the entire land of Cush. The name of the third river is the **Hiddekel**; it runs along the east side of Ashur. And the fourth river is the **Perat**.*"

Consider the two rivers that are called Hiddekel and Perat, as mentioned in Bereshit 2:10-14. Based on where the Tigris and the Euphrates rivers are located today (assuming these are the correct translations for these rivers), most Christians have assumed that the original garden was located somewhere in the Mesopotamian region (around present day Iraq).

However, the Bible records a devastating worldwide flood, many centuries after Adam and Chavah were banned from the Garden. Sedimentary layers, sometimes miles thick, bear testimony to this violent watery devastation which tore apart and buried forever the pre-flood world. After the flood, Noach's family moved to the plain of Shinar (Sumeria/Babylonia) which is where we find rivers today called Tigris and Euphrates. Many believe that these two rivers cannot possibly be the same rivers, because they run on top of Flood-deposited layers of rock. And the Bible speaks of one river breaking into four. This is not what is found in the Middle East today. But we cannot go by what we see today.

We must also consider the fact that the first river that flowed out of Eden is not named, but then splits into the four rivers we know as the lost rivers of Pishon and Gihon, the Tigris (Heddekel) and the Euphrates (Perat) today. It is very likely this first river will not be revealed until Eden reappears because this is where it flows from (so it is hidden as well) and then all will be revealed about where Eden really is.

Where *was* Eden?

There are many who have studied this subject extensively, and have come to the conclusion that the Israel or Lebanon region as the location of Eden and the lost rivers, finds considerable support in the Bible.

Support for this line of reasoning is found in the fact that God considers the land of Israel as His Holy land. It was upon one of the mountains in the *land of Moriah* (Bereshit 22:2) where Abraham was told to sacrifice his son. Solomon was told to build the Temple *at Jerusalem on mount Moriah* (2 Chronicles 3:1). And Jerusalem was where Yeshua was actually crucified.

So we can assume that when God sacrificed an animal to cover Adam and Chavah with its skin (Bereshit 3:21), that animal was a Lamb (Revelation 13:8), and was sacrificed in what we now call Jerusalem. Therefore, we can be certain from the *miqra* (rehearsals) of Adam and Chavah, and the center of the *Garden of God*, were somewhere at or very near the general ***vicinity of Jerusalem - Mount Moriah***. Even the Jews believe that Adam was created from the soil on the Temple Mount - ***Mount Moriah***.

To sum it all up, although the modern-day geology and topography of the Middle-East does not reveal the exact location of the *Garden of Eden*, guidance by faith from the Scriptures and a forensic study of the region's geology reveals the matter. **The available informational facts appear to suggest that present-day Israel, around or in Jerusalem, was the central location of the Garden of Eden.** It will materialize again when Yeshua physically returns to the Earth.

Where is Paradise again?

If you haven't figured it out yet, ***Paradise*** is one and the same as Eden, as in the ***Garden of Eden***. If you have read all the previous chapters, then you can see there is substantial evidence in the Scriptures pointing us to this ***Truth***.

We never actually leave the Earth. All of the facts presented in the previous chapters point to Eden, which may or may not actually be a *place*, in the sense that we know this word - we can now see that **Eden** is something like a ***temporary holding place*** for ***all that is to be restored***, such as the people who have died in Yeshua, ***until the Earth is restored***.

Therefore, we never go to the *Heavens*, **we go to Eden**, and await to be restored with the Earth.   And no one has ever really seen the *Heavens*. Those who claim to have seen or gone to the Heavens, have actually seen or gone to Eden instead (if they really went anywhere at all).

Those family members who believed in Yeshua (or Jesus), are waiting for us in ***Eden*** - **right here on Earth**. And ***Paradise***, which is ***Eden***, is somewhere in the general vicinity of Jerusalem.

In Conclusion

Chapter Ten
In Conclusion

In my studies and in the writing of this book, my views about who goes to *Eden* or not has changed greatly. The Christian (Greek) idea of having to say the correct prayer, or doing the right things or living according to their idea of what a holy life is like, is in extreme error.

We must look at God's pattern in dealing with His people throughout the Hebrew Scriptures. He continually became angry with them, because they simply could not stop being human - and sinful. But then He would give them time to repent and return to Him. But occasionally there were some of these stubborn humans and God knew their hearts could not be swayed to return to Him. Those were the ones we see being punished, killed or even dropped into the abyss alive. They were in rebellion, and rebellion is sin.

There are many people who died who never heard about Yeshua. So what happens to those people? Does God simply toss them aside, assuming they never would have turned to Him?

Although there is the fact that a spirit cannot come back to life without believing in Yeshua, according to John 5:25, 28-29, Romans 15:21, Isaiah 52:15 and 1Peter 4:5-6, even the dead will hear the Good News of Yeshua haMoshiach - and understand it.

So even if someone you know has died without hearing, or understanding what the *Good News* was when they were alive, they will understand it when it is told them on Judgement Day. They will be able to choose, fully understanding what they are being told.

So don't lose heart if someone has unfeelingly told you a loved one went to hell because of this or that reason. If that person was not an evil, rebellious person, know that your loved one will still have the opportunity and choice to believe in Yeshua - their Creator.

In the Name of Yahweh

*"All those who call upon the **Name of Yahweh (or Yeshua)**, will be saved."* This verse is in Joel 2:32 and also in Romans 10:13, but in those verses Yahweh is called *"The Lord."* The Hebrew actually shows YHWH, which is Yahweh in the transliteration, and Romans 10:13 is simply a quote of Joel 2:32.

But His Name is also Yeshua, and if you knew Him only by His altered English Name, Jesus, then you will also be saved if you believe in Him as your Savior.

And when you die you will go to Eden. In Eden you will be with Yeshua, walking through the grass, enjoying the sunshine, and whatever else Eden has to offer. **And when the Earth is restored, God will remove the Cherubim who have been guarding (and hiding) Eden, and we will have access to the Tree of Life again.**

Something to Ponder: Knowing our God and what is really in His Word is so very important in these last days. Please consider searching the Scriptures for the Truth in every area, **instead** of believing and trusting in false teachings.

Resources

Resources

"Holy Bible" - Published by Thomas Nelson Publishers, 1983, NKJV

"One New Man Bible" - Revealing Jewish Roots and Power - Translated by William J. Morford, published 2011

"Interlinear Greek-English New Testament" by George Ricker Berry, originally published 1897

"The Stone Edition Tanach" by Artscroll - the Hebrew Bible (English-Hebrew) as translated by Jewish scribes

"The New Strong's Exhaustive Concordance of the Bible" by James Strong - A concordance of all Biblical words, both Hebrew and Greek.

"Let This Mind Be In You" by Bradford Scott - published first in 2000 - a short historical study of the differences between Greek and Hebrew thought.

"Hebrew Word Pictures" by Dr. Frank T. Seekins - a prophetic look at the ancient Hebrew letters of Yeshua's day, and their true meanings (**A *must have* book**!)

"The Lost Book of Enoch" by Joseph B. Lumpkin - (Enoch 1) - gives us more insight into what caused the flood in Noach's day.

"I AM the WAY, The Essentials of God's Way: The Last Move of God" by Paulette Chartrand published 2014, Second Edition. The most comprehensive and innovative book on the essentials of God's *Way* today. A very thorough study through the Scriptures to discover God's *Way*.

Salvation

Salvation

God knew what would happen to mankind and the earth, so He already had a *Plan*. A *Plan* not only to glorify Himself, but also to save all mankind from themselves - and sin. His original intention was to live among mankind, loving them, enjoying them and all their different personalities, giving them eternal life and the desires of their hearts, and giving them *Free Will* to choose to worship Him - their Creator.

When Adam and Eve were first created, their spirits were alive and connected to God, meaning they were spiritually alive, and thus eternal beings. When God told them they would die if they ate from the *Tree of Knowledge of Good and Evil*, **He meant their spirits would die and be disconnected from Him**, and thus they would no longer be eternal beings.

But they were deceived by the devil, and ate from the tree anyway. This act of disobedience grieved God more than mankind will ever know, for God loves His creation so much, and He created all of mankind to love and worship Him. But He also gave mankind *Free Will*, so they had a choice.

Evil was already in our world because of the *angel rebellion* that took place before Adam and Eve were ever created. Because of this evil, the very first two human beings chose death. Left to their own devices, mankind will always choose destruction.

Because of this choice Adam and Chavah made, all mankind is now born disconnected from God.

Sin is not to be taken lightly - it is a serious matter to God. Because of what Adam and Eve did, **all mankind is born into this world as sinners**, which means we are separated from God from the day we are born.

God wants us all to be rejoined to Him, because He loves each and everyone of us. He made a way for us to be reconnected to Him. He loves us so much, He came down to earth as His Messiah, Yeshua. And then He took all mankind's sin onto Himself as the *first lamb, and* as the *second lamb* of Yom Kippur, He died on the cross. When He did this, He took all mankind's sin to death with Him - destroying it forever. *He brought His Own Blood* to the altar in the *Heavens* to atone for all mankind's sins, because only His Holy Blood could do that for us. At the same time, Yeshua sealed His Blood Covenant with mankind.

BUT, then *He was raised from the dead*, defeating death. That same *Power* that raised Yeshua from the dead can live inside us! And does live inside each person who invites Him into their lives and hearts - and allows Him to be their Savior, Father and Shepherd over their lives. You are either a slave to sin and headed for eternal destruction, or you are a slave to Yeshua headed for eternal life with Him.

That Power that raised Yeshua from the dead is God's Spirit. When invited, for He will never force Himself on you, Yeshua's Spirit will come and dwell inside you to envelope your own spirit with His Life-giving Spirit, causing your spirit to *rise from the dead*. Your spirit literally comes back to life again, which is called *born from above* (some call it *born again*).

Your spirit coming back to life again is <u>not a belief system</u> - it is a *scientific fact*. Simply changing your belief system will not save you from your sins. Going to church will not save you. Being baptized will not save you. Doing these things are simply outward signs that you have chosen to believe in Yeshua, but they cannot save you from your sins. **You will still spend eternity in hell if you do not believe in your heart that Yeshua is the Messiah and Savior, and invite Him into your life.**

Salvation may sound complicated, but to receive this **FREE gift of Life** is actually quite easy. All you do is repent of your sins, **believe that Yeshua bought redemption for you with His Own Blood, and ask Him to forgive you. Then invite Him into your life and heart.** Anyone can do this.

Sidebar: Yeshua, who is Yahweh God, had to use His Own Blood to expiate sin from mankind because blood is tied to creation.

God made it very easy, so no one has to go to hell. **God does not send anyone to hell**, people do that all by themselves by rejecting the only *Way* (door) to *Eternal Life* He has given us - *Yeshua* is that *Way*.

It is Yeshua Who actually becomes our righteousness, holiness and Eternal Life before God when we invite Him to come live inside us.

It is not a matter of whether or not you are good, it is a matter of being able to be in the presence of God. If you have sin in you, then you will not be able to live in the presence of God simply because His very nature will literally kill you.

He is a holy God, and therefore one must be holy to be able to stand in His presence. Unholiness or unrighteousness will die in the presence of God, not because He is a mean God, but because it is His nature. Just as fire has a nature to consume anything it comes in contact with, *our God is also a literal consuming fire and anything unholy that comes in contact with Him will die*.

God wants each and every one of us to choose *His free gift of Life* so that we can come into eternity with Him. He wants us to choose Life. He wants us to choose Yeshua because He is the One Who will Shield us in His presence - we can stand before God because of Yeshua. **Choose Life, choose Yeshua.**